The Our Father

FRANCISCAN SPIRITUALITY: NO. II

By the same author:
UNION WITH CHRIST

The Our Father

By Leo Veuthey, O.F.M. Conv.
Translated by James Meyer, O.F.M.

261
VE

FRANCISCAN HERALD PRESS
Publishers of Franciscan Literature
CHICAGO 9, ILLINOIS

NIHIL OBSTAT:

>CONRADIN WALLBRAUN, O.F.M.
>MARION HABIG, O.F.M.
>*Censores librorum*

IMPRIMI POTEST:

>PIUS J. BARTH, O.F.M.
>*Minister Provincial*

IMPRIMATUR:

>† SAMUEL CARDINAL STRITCH
>*Archbishop of Chicago*

February 2, 1955

Library of Congress Catalog Card Number: 55-5745

1434 WEST 51ST STREET, CHICAGO 9, ILLINOIS
COPYRIGHT, 1955, FRANCISCAN HERALD PRESS
MADE IN THE UNITED STATES OF AMERICA

Foreword

SPEAKING OF ST. FRANCIS at prayer, his first biographer, Thomas of Celano, uses a brilliant expression. He says Francis was no longer a person saying prayers, but a person become prayer.

He had become prayer by the expression seen in his glance, his hands, his countenance and all his members, which, mute in speech but so much the more eloquent in fact, spoke their adoration, entreaty, love and self-devotion. When a person just says prayers, he recites set formulas with more or less purpose and attention. But when he "becomes prayer," he grasps the sense of his prayer and shows that fact involuntarily in his exterior.

Which is to say that prayer consists far more in our way of life, in a state of soul, in a frame of mind than in formulas. And still, when his followers begged him to teach them how to pray, Francis made no other reply at all than what Jesus addressed to his disciples when they put him the same request.

"When you pray," said Francis, who in every-thing wished only to imitate Christ and the Gospel perfectly, "say: Our Father, who are in Heaven, hallowed be your name, your kingdom come, your will be done on earth as it is in Heaven. Give us this day our daily bread, and forgive us our trespasses, as we forgive those who trespass against us, and lead us not into tempta-tion, but deliver us from evil. Amen."

That is the most beautiful formula of prayer ever taught to human beings.

But it is evident that neither Jesus nor his imitator Francis meant to reduce prayer to a formula however beautiful. How else could the words of Jesus that we must always pray (Lk. 18, 1) be reconciled with the words he addressed to his disciples precisely at the moment he was teaching them the Our Father (Mt. 6, 7 on):

"In praying, do not multiply words, as the Gentiles do, who think they will be heard if they use a great many words. Do not be like them, for your Father knows what you need before you ask him."

How are we to pray always without multiply-ing words? Is not that as much as to say that prayer consists much more in a frame of mind than in words? Indeed, in the formula taught by Jesus it is not so much the words which he emphasizes as the enduring spiritual disposition which they are to produce in the person praying, the sumtotal of the sentiments, aspirations and desires which constitute the essence of prayer and which can and should constantly animate the human heart.

Moreover, when he taught the Our Father, Jesus was replying to a specific question. The Apostles asked Jesus to teach them how to pray. The Master should really have had to reply with a long explanation on the nature of prayer and the way to pray. Instead, as was his manner, Jesus does not lose himself in abstract explanations but gives a concrete example which in its fulness of meaning contains more than any long treatise on prayer.

Rather than teach us a formula, Jesus wanted to demonstrate in what way we can pray, and pray always; to tell us what sentiments and aspirations should animate us at prayer, what dispositions of mind constitute prayer, constant prayer, prayer such as "makes a person all prayer."

As we study the Our Father, we shall learn from Jesus himself the right way to pray and to shape our prayer. And since prayer is the essence of the interior life, Jesus in teaching us the Our Father will teach us how to practice and live that interior life which is the source of our supernatural elevation, of holiness and of perfect joy. We shall find that to live the interior life is to live the Our Father rather than repeat the formula of it.

Still, if repeating the formula (more fully savored because more fully understood) can help us maintain our soul in the frame of mind which it implies, such repetition will not be opposed to our Lord's precept against multiplying words at our prayer. For if it maintains our soul in the state of prayer, which counts a great deal more than the words, it will serve to realize that other precept of our Lord about praying always.

Contents

Father

I

B Y THE FIRST KEYWORD OF the Our Father, Jesus indicates from the very first what is the proper direction to give to our spirit at prayer. It is up to the Father that our glance must mount at our adoration, our praise, our petition, for he is the Source, the Principle, of everything good, of all life, of all light.

It is from the Father that everything comes forth, it is to the Father that everything must return: "Every excellent gift and every perfect grace descends from on high, from the Father of lights" (Jas. 1, 17).

It is from the Father that the Son himself comes forth, and likewise the procession of the Holy Spirit. It is to the Father that the Son returns in the breath of love of the Holy Ghost, to the Father that everything must return in the Son, the incarnate Word, Jesus Christ with his mystical body, mortal men, and then all

creation. The Father is the beginning and the
end of all things; he is the beginning and the
end of prayer, which is the expression of our
love as well as of our need of love.

Yet how many forget the Father in their
prayer! How many halt at their favorite saint!
How many others go no farther than Jesus, forgetting that Jesus himself teaches us that our
prayer should address itself to the Father and
that it is of the Father that we should ask all
things in his name:

"When you pray, say, Our Father . . ." (Lk.
11, 2). "Pray to your Father in secret" (Mt.
6, 6). "Whatever you ask the Father in my
name that I will do" (Jn. 14, 13). "Amen,
amen, I say to you, if you ask the Father anything in my name, he will give it to you" (Jn.
16, 23).

Does that mean we are not to pray to the
saints, not to pray to Jesus at all? By no means!
On the contrary, that is the way to arrive at the
Father. The saints and the angels convey our
prayers to the Father; but instead of halting at
them as if they were the principle and source,
we should with them and in them, in the communion of the saints, in union with Christ and
his mystical body, mount up to the Father.

Because the Father is the source, the beginning and the end, it is to him our prayer should mount and in him terminate—our petitions as well as our homage, our love, our praise, and our adoration.

To be sure, if Jesus is truly "our advocate with the Father" (1 Jn. 2, 1) , and if he proceeds from the Father and returns to him, then he is also God in unity with the Father and the Holy Ghost, and as such he is also the object of our prayer and our adoration.

Then, too, if he teaches us to ask the Father in his name, he also tells us in a tone of complete equality: "If you ask me for anything in my name, I will give it to you" (Jn. 14, 14) . This particular text is reported in the Gospel of St. John only, who has always in mind the defense of the Divinity of Jesus and his equality with the Father in their one Divine nature.

Nonetheless it remains true that the Father is the source and principle, and that in distinguishing the three persons the order of prayer as well as the order of the Trinity requires that we return to the Father in the Son through the Holy Ghost.

So, let us pray to the saints, let us pray to Christ, but with them and in him let us go on to the Source, to the Father, in whom alone the soul finds its full expansion in the infinite essence of the Trinity, for which it has been created.

How many souls tie themselves down to their nothingness, just vegetate, making no progress, never expanding, because they are locked up in themselves instead of getting in union with Jesus, losing themselves in him, thus expanding in him and returning in him to the Father in the full expanse of the infinite Trinity!

This return to the Father, for that matter, is an experience made by all interior souls. Beginners on the way of perfection readily become attached to some favorite saint. Later, devotion to Mary, the Mother of all the saints, leads all the rest. But in Mary the soul finds Jesus and passes from devotion to Mary and makes the gift of itself to Christ in love and affection which eventually identifies lover and Beloved.

Arrived at that identification, the soul shares in the aspiration of Jesus toward the Father in the Holy Ghost. For a time at least, the soul seems to forget the saints, the Blessed Virgin, yes Jesus himself—to whom however it is more closely joined than ever—to lose itself in the infinite ocean of God in its loving return to the Father, the return, that is, in the breath of the Spirit of Love, which is the Son's relation to the Father.

In the soul become one with the Son, the full consciousness of our Divine childship is realized, sharing in the sonship of the Word, through Jesus and the Holy Spirit, in whom it cries out its love for the Father. As St. Paul says, "You have received the Spirit of adoption, in which we cry Abba, Father" (Rom. 8, 15).

Such is the soul's part in the Son's return to the Father in Love, in the Holy Spirit, in the oneness of the Blessed Trinity, which consists in the mutual gift of Love on the part of the Father to the Son and of the Son to the Father.

"Father!" This is the loving cry of the Son as he returns to the Father in that Love which is the Holy Ghost. Father! It signifies all the life of the Son's infinite and eternal love.

Father! That is the loving cry of the soul become one with the Son in loving identification, in unity with the mystical Christ, as it returns in him to the Source of Love.

Father! It means all the life of man's infinite and eternal love as he shares in the loving life of the Son once he has become a child of the Father by adoption through him who is the eternal Son by nature.

Such interior souls know of that relation, they relish it, they live it, and at times they have no further word to say, no other formula of prayer, but the word uttered by the Son on returning to his Source and Origin: Father! Their life has become a perpetual cry of love: Father!

That cry of love is the soul's very breath, its steady ascent to the Source of Love, where the soul goes to drink in long draughts what constitutes all its joy, all its life. Become one with the Son, the soul shares in the Son's continually being generated by the Father, just as it shares in his eternal aspiration of Love, which becomes his love for the soul in the blessed Trinity and so becomes the soul's life, its all, its joy, its unspeakable bliss.

How many a soul has no need of going any farther in its prayer, in reciting the Our Father! That word is enough for them: Father! That word says everything. It says more than any formulas, because it is the eternal, infinite word of the Son.

It shall be our eternal word in him, a word that spells love, adoration, appreciation, dependence, gift of self, our being generated and returning to him, our life, our participation in the life of the Trinity, and so our perfect joy, our eternal bliss.

Father! That is prayer in its entirety, the essence of prayer in what is most beautiful and sublime about prayer. The interior soul, once

arrived at the consciousness of the reality expressed in the first word of the Our Father, feels
its bond of love with the Father in the Holy
Ghost, its Divine childship in the Son, in whom,
through the Holy Ghost, it utters the word
which expresses all its life, all its being, all its
blessed activity: "Father."

"God has put into our heart the Spirit of his
Son, in whom we cry Abba, Father."

Our Father

II

IN ENTERING THE Our Father among the prayers of the Mass, Mother Church introduces
it with the strange formula: "Admonished
by salutary precepts and instructed by Divine
ordinance we venture to say, Our Father . . ."

1. Is the title Father here so terrible and so
bold a word that we do not dare to say it except
by express Divine command and establishment?
Father! The word is so commonplace that we
address it to God naturally, without being aware
of any such terrible boldness.

Yet, if we gave it a little further thought, how
should we account to ourselves for the boldness
on the part of wretched finite creatures such as
we are, saying "Father" to God, the uncreated,
infinite, eternal Being?

For father and son imply one and the same
nature. Father and son are either both human
beings, or both animals, or both plants. Any

plant can never say father to an animal, nor any
animal to a human being. Indeed, as between
one species of plant and another, or one species
of animal and another, any fatherhood relation
is impossible.

Yet plant, animal and man are finite creatures,
subject to matter, space and time; while the difference between one species of plant and another, or between one species of animal and
another is even slighter, but that slight difference makes it impossible for one ever to say
father to the other.

Between God and man, on the other hand,
there is an infinite difference and distance. And
man dares to say "Father" to God! Yes indeed,
that is a great stroke of boldness, and it truly
needed a Divine command to permit it.

Only the Word, the only Son, Jesus, the Christ,
can say Father to God. So if Jesus teaches us
to say Father likewise, it can only be because
we are somehow one with him and are incorporated with him. It is only because we form
a single mystical body with him, one only son,
that we can say—in him!—"Father."

And that is why we say *"Our* Father"—"our,"
that is to say, the Father of Jesus and of me who
am praying in him and can say "Father" only

inasfar as I am in him and form a unit with him
and we are "two in one flesh," one sole mystical
body.

Our Father! It is in Jesus alone that I can say
that, inasmuch as I share in his Divine childship,
in the Divine nature in him, and have thus become in him, by sharing and adoption of the
same nature as the Father, a member of the
family of God.

That is the grand law of prayer taught by the
Our Father: we cannot pray in a worthy manner
except in Jesus, uniting ourselves with him and
becoming one with him. That is why Jesus
keeps repeating so often that we must ask the
Father for everything in his name. Just that is
the condition on which our prayer will be heard
and answered: "Nobody comes to the Father
except through me (Jn. 14, 6) ; everything that
you ask of the Father in my name he will give
it to you (Jn. 16, 23) ; whatever you ask the
Father in my name, I will do" (Jn. 14, 13) .

More still, whatever we ask of Jesus as God,
it is only in Jesus as the Word incarnate that we
can ask it: "If you ask anything of me in my
name, I will do it" (Jn. 14, 14) .

Do we understand now why there is no other
way to get to God, to the Father, except by

uniting ourselves with Jesus, and becoming one
with him through grace, love, intention, and
constant communion?

Do we understand now that there is no other
way to pray, and to pray well, except by uniting
ourselves with Jesus, causing our prayer to be
the prayer of Jesus in us, the prayer of his Spirit,
who "helps our weakness; for we do not know
for what we should pray as we ought, but the
Spirit himself pleads for us with unutterable
groanings" (Rom. 8, 26).

What consolation too this is for those who at
a certain point in their life find themselves
unable to pray, even after Holy Communion.
Happy lack of ability, for then Jesus himself
wishes in the Spirit to take over for us and be
our prayer!

Oh, at such times let us unite ourselves blindly
with Jesus, let us disappear in him, so that he
can be our prayer, our adoration, our praise,
our thanksgiving. Let us offer ourselves up in
him, in union with him, and in union with his
intentions, which will in him become our intentions; in union with his prayer, which will
thus become our prayer, a prayer far more perfect than all our finest words and all our best
sentiments.

How well we can thus understand the words

of a soul which experienced that inability:
"After Communion I am unable to pray, so I say
to Jesus: You yourself be my act of thanksgiving!" The Eucharist—by its very name, is it not
thanksgiving by excellence?

And how can we thank the Father more perfectly for the infinite gift he accords us than by
making him the infinite gift of his Son, in offering him the infinitely perfect prayer which is
his Son?

And in turn what better way to thank the Son
himself than in giving ourself altogether to him,
annihilating ourself in him, so that he can be
our love, our all, our life, our prayer, our adoration, our meed of praise? Is it not the way of
great love that the lover loses himself in the
Beloved?

2. *Our* Father! The word thus expresses our
communion or association with Jesus at our
prayer. But it likewise expresses our association with the "complete Jesus," the "entire
Christ," the mystical body of Christ, in the loving communion of all his members, of every
soul, in him.

There is no effectual prayer, no supernatural
prayer except in Christ. But Christ is one with
all his members, and it is only in living in this
unity that we shall live in him, and it is only

in praying in this unity that we shall pray in
him. Thus we never do pray alone, but always
along with Jesus and with all our brethren in
him—in the name of Jesus and in the name of
our brethren.

That puts the ban on all egoism. It is charity
triumphing by means of that unity which has us
say in union with Jesus and with all our brethren
in him "Our Father," and not *"my* Father."

To pray alone, in one's own name, for oneself
only—that would be to isolate ourself from
Christ and from the glorious loving unity of all
mankind in him and through him in God. "God
is love, and he who abides in love, abides in
God, and God abides in him" (1 Jn. 4, 16).

When we say *Our* Father, we live in God's
love and God lives in us.

That life in love and charity with all our
brethren, in the unity of Christ, is so necessary
to prayer, to prayer in Jesus, that he himself
tells us that if anything separates us from our
brothers, our prayer or our sacrifice cannot be
accepted by God. He wishes that we be first
reconciled with our brother before coming to
present our offering at the altar:

"If you are offering your gift at the altar and
there remember that your brother has anything
against you, leave your gift before the altar and

go first to be reconciled with your brother, and then come and offer your gift" (Mt. 5, 23-24).

What then must be said of those who present themselves at Communion, at Mass, at prayer, with hatred in their heart after having offended their brother! God does not hear such people, because they are separated from unity with the mystical Christ inasmuch as they are separated from that brother who is Christ in one of his members. Thus they cannot pray in Christ and in the name of Christ.

Let them first go and be reconciled with their brother, let them rid themselves of their hatred and of all rancor. For then will they be in Christ, in union with him and with God through love.

If prayer means elevating the soul to God and being in communion with God in the love which is God, it is clear that there can be no worthy prayer apart from love and charity.

When we say *"Our* Father" in loving communion with Jesus and our brethren, we also enter into loving communion with the Father in the Holy Ghost. Oh, if only all people prayed the Our Father sincerely, how changed everything on earth would be! Universal brotherhood would truly have arrived. No more war, no more strife and contention, but union of

everybody in Christ under the blessing regard of
the Father, charity prevailing, with mutual tol-
erance, harmony, and exchange of help, sharing
one another's joys and finding common solace
in misfortune.

It would mean the beginning of Paradise.

If that universal paradise on earth must always remain an ideal without ever turning into
reality, let every man at least seek to realize it
in his own heart by saying the Our Father in
all its significance of love, charity, and amity, so
that on our lips the dear word "Father" truly
means that we are living with our brothers in
Jesus—in Jesus, who alone can say that word
speaking for himself as well as speaking within
us for us. For it is the same word "Father" which
expresses the eternal loving return which the
Son makes to his Source in loving union with the
Holy Spirit, in that intimate interchange of love
which is the Holy Trinity.

Saying the word "Father" in Jesus, we partici-
pate, in him and in union with every soul in
him, in that eternal loving return. We partici-
pate passively and actively in the spiration of
the Holy Spirit, who is that love in which the
Father begets the Son and the Son returns to the
Father, in that loving life of the Trinity which
is perfect joy, happiness and bliss.

It is the essence of that love which we keep seeking, but in vain, in everything and everywhere on this earth, because it can be found in God alone, by sharing in his loving life.

Any other love is only a fleeting shadow of that master Love which nevertheless we are in a measure called to share even here on earth, in Christ, in union with all our brethren, as we share in common Divine Charity.

Who are in Heaven

III

PRAYER CONSISTS in raising the soul to God. But since man is both spirit and matter, man experiences a two-fold spontaneous but contrary movement in himself. The material part of him with all its senses follows its natural tendency and deadweight toward material things, things subject to the senses, especially to feeling, toward whatever is of this earth and of the flesh.

In turn, the spiritual part of man with its faculties, the understanding and the will, ought naturally to tend toward the spiritual, toward the higher things, toward God.

But in his fallen nature the material part of man often prevails over the spiritual, smothers and crushes it with its weight, so that man inclines more toward the material and the objects of the senses and feelings than to what is spiritual and divine.

19

Now, prayer is action of the spirit that supplies counterweight to the tendency of the flesh. While the latter tends downward, prayer causes the soul to turn upward again, lifts the soul back on high, toward God and Heaven.

Prayer is elevation of the soul, returning it to its natural pole, to the goal and destination of everything spiritual.

There are people who would say prayer consists in lovely sentiments, fine formulas, long-drawn utterances. But prayer is something far more simple: it is just elevating the soul, having it go back to the things on high, having it associate with God.

Sentiments, formularies, extended speech may serve that purpose, and indeed they have no value except inasfar as they help that elevation.

But formulas and words are not necessary to the essence of prayer. A glance heavenward, toward God, a sigh, a desire however vague and undefined but yet directed toward the fountain-head of all desire, toward God, who is Love— all that is prayer, for it makes a reality of elevation of the soul as it adores or implores, or gives thanks or repents.

It is, too, the only way in which our Lord's precept can be made a reality, "You should pray

always." We cannot go on saying prayer formulas all day, but we can keep our soul directed
heavenward, even in the midst of intellectual
and material labors; and that not only by means
of a good intention to sanctify everything and
transform our occupations into prayer, but also
by habitual contact with God, by thus keeping
our sight habitually directed toward God as the
silent accompaniment of all our attentions to
everyday affairs, making them all end up in God.

Yes, there comes a point in the spiritual life
when the soul's glance never again gives up its
hold on God.   Not all souls arrive at that point,
but all should strain toward it, first of all by
often renewing their good intention, their touch,
their communion with God, their actual regard
of him, and then with the grace of God renewing
their thought of him so often that it becomes a
steady habit, habitual elevation, continuous
prayer.

In that way, purified of the effects of the Fall,
the soul will recover its natural tendency toward
God and its supernatural association with God.
It will rid itself of the burden of matter which
weighs it down and of sensuality which suffocates
it, so that it can live the life of love for which
it was made and fly up continually toward its

"place," its nest, its goal and destination—
toward Heaven, the Father, the blessed Trinity,
and its interchange of light and love with the
Divine.

Thus it is to indicate the essence of prayer
and put us from the first in the atmosphere of
prayer that Jesus teaches us to begin by turning
our glance toward the "Father" and toward
"Heaven." How many souls there are that have
no need of going any farther in order to pray
truly, to live in prayer, in contemplation!

The two words Father, Heaven, suffice to steep
them in it, to plunge them into a divine bath,
the bath of the light and love of the blessed
Trinity!

Aided by his imagination and following the
analogy with the material heavens, man is led
to look for God and his Heaven beyond the
starry firmament. When therefore he says, "Our
Father, who are in Heaven," his sight naturally
turns to the azure sky, and he seeks to penetrate
what looks to him like the reverse side of
Heaven.

Though that is just a play of imagination, it
can be a help to beginners in lifting their soul
up to God. At that, it expresses in the order
of the senses the spiritual fact of Heaven and
of God. God actually is superior to all things

and beyond them all, but with the reality of the
spiritual, which has nothing to do with space
(for space is material). God's being above and
beyond all things is not in the realm of the
material but of the spirit.

Still, interior souls have their experience of
this spiritual existence of God and of Heaven.
Yet it is not in distant space, beyond the starry
firmament, that they find God, but within themselves, in the depth of their soul. There is "the
kingdom of Heaven," which is "within us." As
Jesus has said: "The kingdom of God is within
you" (Lk. 17, 21).

It is the kingdom of the interior life, which
is the lot of those who know how to disengage
themselves from the slavery of the senses, from
the material, from all this base, idle, transient,
passing external activity, since the soul has need
of higher things, which are fully real in value,
and changeless, and eternal. It is in withdrawing
from the external world, from space and time,
and entering into itself that the soul finds all
that, finds everything it needs.

Says St. Augustine: "Do not go outdoors for
him; he dwells in you. Lord, my Lord, I looked
for you outside of me, whereas you were within
me!"

He is within us, yet nevertheless above and

beyond us. But our soul is the path and the gateway to that region beyond, to that Heaven, where God dwells. If he is beyond us and still always within us, it is because our soul opens out upon the Infinite; because by means of grace and our sharing in the Divine nature, in the very being of God and of the blessed Trinity, our soul transcends itself, sharing in the Infinite and thus finding the Infinite, finding God and the blessed Trinity within itself, for it is in God itself, and shares there in the blessed Trinity's action of Light and Love.

That is the kingdom of the interior life, the abode of the Father, the Heaven, to which prayer elevates us, the temple of the Holy Ghost, the domain of the Trinity.

Thus the soul in the state of grace is not just "a little heaven" distinct from "the great Heaven," but it is Heaven itself through the soul's elevation into the Infinite by means of its sharing in the very being of God.

Oh, that we might lose ourself by being lost in God, in the infinite Ocean of Light and Love, the Ocean of the interior life!

If therefore at the outset of the interior life the soul feels the need of withdrawing into itself and away from all the outer world in order to find God, there comes the time too where it becomes aware of its infinite character through partaking of the Divine; where it no longer feels only that God is within it, but also that it is in the midst of God, in God, "in the center of the Godhead," to use the words of the Franciscan mystics Bl. Angela of Foligno and St. Veronica Giuliani.

Then the soul no longer advances from the creatures to God, but it sees and perceives God in all the creatures and all the creatures in God, as St. Bonaventure says.

To advance from the creature to God is still following the order of nature. But steeped in the supernatural, the soul sees everything in God and so sees everything in its unity. And since it shares this unity itself, it bathes in it and enjoys it with greater or lesser clearness or obscurity in the spiritual, mystical life, while awaiting the enjoyment of the perfect clearness of eternity.

In having us begin our prayer with the words "Our Father, who are in Heaven," Jesus wished to lift our soul up and make us realize as a result of this uplift the very essence of prayer. He wanted to withdraw us from the exterior world, in order to have us enter the kingdom of the interior life, the kingdom of Heaven.

He himself is that kingdom. In him our soul shares in the nature of God and his triune life, which constitutes Paradise. Entering into itself, the soul enters into the kingdom of Heaven. It returns to the "Father," who is in Heaven. It shares in the intellectual generation of the Word and in the loving spiration of the Holy Ghost. It lives in God, in the bosom of the blessed Trinity.

That is the idea of prayer, the beauty of prayer. Not everybody will rise to awareness of this beauty, this joy, this Divine mystery of the Infinite. There is the imperfection which attends beginners, there are the moments of dryness and darkness.

But all can live the life by means of faith. All can, even in this world—by means of faith, recollection and good intention, if not by ineffable mystical experience—live the fact of the interior life, the mystery of that prayer which unites us with our Father who is in Heaven, through union with the Son in the breath of the Light and Love of the Holy Ghost.

Why tie ourselves down in prayer to the wretched mechanical recitation of formulas when these very formulas are designed to raise us to such heights?

Hallowed be Your Name

IV

USUALLY PEOPLE CONFUSE the terms prayer and petition. It is done to the extent that many have no idea at all of prayer except as a request for help and relief. What is still more, the request for help and relief is reduced oftenest to the material, temporal interests of the person offering the prayer.

How different is what Jesus teaches us about prayer. To him it is not a self-centered request for material goods, but it is above all reaching out to God, praise of God.

1. Thus the first petition of the Our Father is not directed toward ourselves but toward God and his glory: "Hallowed be your name!" The center and aim of our prayer, like the center and aim of our life, should not be ourself but our Lord. And really it is only in forgetting ourself that we find our Lord.

What must be said therefore of people who

turn prayer into a sort of wretched self-worship, such as centers on self and self-interest? Of people to whom God is only a means in the service of their ego, whereas their ego should be subordinated to the service and glory of God?

Jesus does not forbid us to pray also for our own needs, but he would have us do so first of all for our spiritual needs. Thus, when he teaches us to ask for our daily bread, he has above all the spiritual bread of the soul in mind and only secondarily everything that is to serve our material needs.

And these needs, moreover, we need not specify, since God knows what they are even before we ask for them. Indeed, he knows better than we of what we stand in need and what is good for us.

All the rest of the petitions of the Our Father likewise have reference to our spiritual needs— as to forgive our trespasses, not to let us succumb to temptation, to deliver us from evil.

If, therefore, in the second part of the Our Father, Jesus permits us as a secondary point of our prayer to think of ourselves, first—note again —it is not in any selfish fashion, by putting our own individual self in the foreground, but in the charitable terms of "us," causing the request to be more for our neighbor than for ourselves.

And then, it is still no less true that all the first part of the Our Father, which is the most sublime part of it and the most important in the order and range of prayer—all of it is directed toward God and refers to him.

In other words, God should be the center and object of our prayer, and not we ourselves. Prayer is above all an act of homage to God, of adoration, of praise.

That is what the first petition of the Our Father expresses: "Hallowed be your name." It means, may your name be adored all over the world, may it be praised and glorified, may everything sing its praise. So, it is not of ourselves that Jesus teaches us to think in our prayer, but above all of God and his glory.

The aim of prayer, therefore, are the four purposes for which the holy Mass is offered— the prayer by excellence. Now, the purposes of the sacrifice are above all praise and adoration of God together with gratitude and thanksgiving toward him, accompanied by expiation and petition. And the very first petition of the Our Father is precisely praise and adoration along with gratitude and thanksgiving: "May your name be sanctified, glorified, adored, and gratefully appreciated by all your creatures."

A cry of love, of adoration, of grateful ac-

knowledgement—such is the significance of these
words, which so many people recite mechanically
whereas their soul ought to be dilating in one
long, living breath of praise at the most sublime
petition of the Our Father: Hallowed be your
name!

Your name—that means, in the language of
the East and of the Bible, the reality, the person
itself, God, who has created everything for his
glory, to be loved by creation and adored by
creation.

2. Truly interior souls feel this call of man
to sing eternally the glory of God, as do the
saints in Heaven with their eternal "Holy, holy,
holy." Sister Elizabeth of the Trinity found this
vocation revealed to her on reading the words of
St. Paul, according to which God has created us
"in laudem gloriae—for the praise of his glory,"
and she wanted thereafter to be called just that—
"Praise of Glory."

Praise of Glory—that can and ought be the
name of everyone of us, since it is the vocation
of all of us, since it is for his glory that God
has created us.

The interior soul, rid of all self-interest, finds
all its joy in forgetting itself in order to think
only of the glory of the Beloved, the glory of
God, which it would love to sing with every

fiber of its being; which it would love to pro-
mote by every means with every drop of its
blood; which it would love to hear and have
sung by all men, all creatures, every last thing,
as does the inspired singer with his hymns and
psalms, which the interior soul loves to repeat
after him:

> All you works of the Lord, bless the Lord,
> Praise and exalt him forever.

> You angels of the Lord, bless the Lord,
> Praise and exalt him forever.

> You heavens, bless the Lord,
> Praise and exalt him forever.

> You waters and everything above the heavens,
> bless the Lord,
> Praise and exalt him forever.

> All you powers of the Lord, bless the Lord,
> Praise and exalt him forever.

> Sun and moon, praise the Lord,
> Praise and exalt him forever.

> You stars of heaven, bless the Lord,
> Praise and exalt him forever.

> You rains and dews, bless the Lord,
> Praise and exalt him forever.

> All you winds of God's hand, bless the Lord,
> Praise and exalt him forever.

>   —Dan. 3, 57-65.

And, continuing with the inspired singer, the
soul goes on inviting fire and heat, and cold and

warm weather, and mists and rime, and frosts
and freezing weather, and ice and snows, nights
and days, light and darkness, all the earth, to
bless the Lord.

Mountains and hills, all the plants, the springs,
the seas and the rivers, the fishes in the waters
and the birds of the sky, all beasts wild and tame,
young men and old, priests and servants of God,
the spirits and the souls of the just, the saints
and the humble of heart—praise the Lord and
exalt him forever.

Again the interior soul loves to sing with the
psalmist:

> Praise God from the heavens; praise him from
> out of the heights.

> Praise him, all you angels, praise him, all you
> his hosts.

> Praise him, sun and moon; praise him, all you
> twinkling stars.

—Ps. 148, 1-5.

Together with the psalmist it goes on thus
inviting all the beings of the heavens, of the
earth, and of all the universe to sing the praise
of the Lord.

It is that same inspiration, that same sense of
the soul's vocation to sing the glory of God and
to have it sung by all creation which carried St.
Francis away to compose the *Canticle of Brother*

Sun, and wish his brothers to go out into the streets and public places and the towns and countrysides to chant the praises of the Lord and be "the troubadours and jugglers of God."

"Hallowed be your name." In this first petition of the Our Father the interior soul thus expresses all its vocation "to praise his glory," all its priestly office of speaking for all creation and singing the glory of the Most High. Therein it finds something to nourish all its prayers, all its life, its very eternity, in a sea of joy, love, adoration and thanksgiving.

The motto "to praise his glory," says all that in one breath. It becomes so to say the life and breath of the soul made for the praise of God, for love, adoration and thanksgiving, and all its joy, its happiness, its infinite bliss are drawn from that source.

In that source the soul finds its perfection, for it finds that all its activity and all its behavior even more so than whatever it says, must become praise of his glory to the Lord. And what holiness, what perfection of life is not required so that our conduct and all our activity at every instant prove to be praise of our Lord's glory? Let those souls tell of that who have grasped the idea of their vocation to praise his glory.

The interior soul, thus, never forgets that it

has the vocation to glorify God and give spiritual voice to all the material voices of nature in order to have them mount as a hymn of praise to God, who is spirit.

Just so, it does not forget that its own voice cannot mount up to God and cannot honor him worthily except when it joins with the voice of the Godman Christ; for he summarizes in himself all the voices of the universe as the Mediator and Priest in whom all things mount up to God in order to sing his glory and praise in the Holy Spirit.

It is therefore only in union with Christ, in Christ and his Spirit of Love, that man can utter and live this petition, just like all the other petitions, of the Our Father. It is in Christ only that man's prayer mounts up to God in the Divine prayer of Christ, who above all else in the sacrifice of the Mass is the perfect offering of praise and adoration, the oblation of God to God, the praise of God for God, the Love of God for God. And in that praise and love Christ is the praise and love offered by man, and of all creatures in man.

But it is praise which is transformed, praise rendered infinite and divine, and thus worthy of God—the hymn of praise given by the incarnate Son to the Father in the perfect sacrifice of love.

Your Kingdom Come

V

THE FIRST OF THE SEVEN petitions of the Our Father has God alone as its final object. That is absolutely the contrary of the idea too commonly held of prayer, which makes the object and aim of it oneself and one's own needs. It is the direct opposite of that egoism which thinks only of itself, whereas Jesus means to teach us charity and forgetfulness of self.

He teaches us that first of all we should think of God and his glory, of praising and loving God.

Such disinterestedness is the essential condition to make our prayer perfect. Indeed it is the condition of man's own perfection, for he does not attain to his goal, to supernatural perfection, to holiness, except on the condition that he forgets about himself, makes nothing of himself, loses himself in God, forgetting about himself in order to be mindful only of God and his glory.

Interior souls understand that—they whom all

their prayer little by little detaches from personal interests and the thought of themselves in
order to leave them occupied only with the interests of God, so that he and his glory and praise
are all they think of. There is no perfection except at that price.

Souls preoccupied with themselves are vic-
tims of their selfishness, but God is found only
in victory over all egoism, in the death of self in
all its forms, so that it can lose and find itself
again in the person of God. The interior soul
detached from selfishness and from its own ego,
lives thereafter for God and his glory alone. In
that it finds its boundless joy, its true life, the
life which corresponds with its infinite needs of
the Divine.

1. Now, the second petition of the Our Father
is the perfect example of this loss of our ego in
order to find it again transformed, enlarged,
made divine in God. Still, if the first petition re-
ferred altogether to God, the second has its
reference to us and our happiness, the matter
which concerns us most and is the goal of all
our life.

But again, in having us ask for it, Jesus teaches
us here again to forget about ourselves in order
to think only of God, since he has us plead not

for our paradise but for his kingdom. It is in the death of all egoism that we shall find perfect life, happiness, paradise. "Your kingdom come!"

The kingdom of God—that evidently is paradise, Heaven, our paradise, our heaven, our happiness. Only we do not pray for these blessings as ours—that again would be egoism and self-seeking.

No, we pray for them as things belonging to God, as matters of glory and satisfaction to God; that God may have his reign over the blessed spirits and enjoy triumph in his creature world, enjoy the glory it affords him in his kingdom.

Thus it is a continuation of the first petition, of our desire for the glory of God. But again, it is in being above all selfishness and in giving the first place to God that our deepest desire, the desire of eternal bliss and happiness, is realized.

For man can be happy only in the happiness of God. When he pleads for the happiness of God in having his kingdom realized, it is the realization of his own happiness which man wins for himself.

The kingdom of God was the cry of hope and longing voiced by all the Old Testament as it awaited the coming of the Messiah, who was to bring it about. It is likewise the goal of all the

New Testament, which teaches the way to the kingdom of God, lays the foundations for it, and begins its realization.

It is, too, the ardent desire of all interior souls, who see no other goal for their life but the realization of God's kingdom.

Your kingdom come! Rule over me, O my God. Be my All. Let me lose myself and become as nothing in you. Rule over all souls, over all mankind, over all creatures. Let there be an end to the reign of evil, of sin, of the Evil Spirit, of the flesh, of matter. May you alone reign supreme in everything, and be served, adored, thanked, praised and extolled in song by all things forever!

2. That kingdom of God, perfect in unity and order, with all things in perfect submission and return to the Source of all joy and bliss—it is plainly the Heaven or the Paradise of eternity. As Jesus has said (Jn. 18, 36), "My kingdom is not of this world."

For that union of all things in God through love, and that perfect order through submission of all things to God, that happiness and perfect joy—all that is evidently not of this world.

It was the mistake of the Jews that they believed the kingdom of the Messiah would be realized on earth. In the same way so many

people of our day make the mistake of believing
they can realize paradise on earth and satisfy
here below man's unslakeable thirst for justice
and happiness.

Paradise is not a matter of this world. It is
realized in the beyond. And trying to realize it
in this world while overlooking the beyond, is
to run the risk of losing the one and the other.

Paradise is an ideal toward which we must
keep forever striving, but the full realization of
it cannot be had until beyond. Still, by striving
for it steadily, we succeed in realizing it to a certain point already in this world. That is why
Jesus, who says his kingdom is not of this world,
also says (Lk. 17, 21), "The kingdom of God is
within you."

Then, what is that kingdom of God which is
not of this world and still is within us even in
this life? What is that kingdom which Jesus
teaches us to pray for as the kingdom of his
Father—"Your kingdom come!"—and which at
the same time he calls "my kingdom" (Lk. 22,
30; Jn. 18, 36)?

It is his kingdom within us, the kingdom of
Jesus in our midst. It is Jesus in our midst, Jesus
himself who was in the midst of his disciples and
said to them, "Behold, the kingdom of God is
within you."

It is Jesus, who at the Last Supper pleaded with the Father that his kingdom might be realized, when he pleaded that all his own should be joined in one great unity with him, so that they might be one in him and through him one with the Father (Jn. 17, 21-23) :

"Yet, not for these only do I pray, but for those also who through their word will believe in me, that all may be one, just as you, Father, in me and I in you; that they also may be one in us . . . that they may be one just as we are one, I in them, and you in me; that they may be perfect in unity."

The kingdom of God within us is therefore Jesus in us—"I in them"—and the kingdom of the Father means we being in Jesus, we being one in him and through him, and so one in the Father through the oneness of the love of the Holy Spirit—"one in us."

It is a kingdom which begins in this world and will be made perfect in the next world; which begins for each one of us at our baptism, at the moment we are incorporated in Christ, the moment we begin to live in him and through him, the moment of the entry of all the Trinity into us and of our entry into the Trinity.

That kingdom becomes perfect in each of us in the measure that Jesus takes more and more full possession of us; that "he increases and we decrease"; that he ends by taking over all the room we shall give him as the result of humbling and mortifying ourselves, mortifying our nature and its tendencies, and renouncing everything else as well as our ego, our selfishness and our pride, so that he alone may live in us and we can say, "Now not I live, but Jesus lives in me" (Gal. 2, 20).

As this incorporation and transformation advances in all souls that have given themselves to Christ, all become one in him, and through him one in the Father, each one possessing the kingdom entirely, that is, possessing Jesus entirely, yet all of them forming in him a single kingdom, just as every host in all the tabernacles of the world contains the entire Christ and still all of them are just one single Christ, the Son of the Father.

This realization of the kingdom goes into effect even in this world, "in our midst," through the union of the Mystical Body, the Church, the union of all those incorporated in Christ, of all the members of Christ; but the kingdom, the body of Christ, the Church does not reach its full, external achievement till in the next world.

The kingdom is not of this world, but it is in our midst. And who does not see that if it were

in each and everyone of us, in the internal and
external unity of the Church Militant, Jesus
would be reigning also in this world?

He would be having there the royal palace to
which he has a right and would be establishing
peace, justice and charity there. For peace, justice and charity will reign in the world in the
same measure that God's reign is established in
each one of us.

The kingdom of God is not of this world.
Paradise is for beyond. But in striving for it even
in this world, we succeed in realizing it even
here below, each person in himself and all of
us in the world at large, in the unity of the
Church and the unity of charity.

That is the same as to say that every one of
us can work to realize the kingdom of Heaven
in the world by realizing it first of all in himself. In saying, "Your kingdom come," the interior soul is pleading for Paradise, for the
perfect reign of the Father in his Son, in his
Mystical Body at large, for that is the kingdom
of God and of Christ in the world.

But the soul knows that it must first realize
the kingdom of the Father and of the Son in
union with the Holy Ghost in its own internal
kingdom by transforming itself perfectly into
Christ, becoming altogether one with him, by

sharing, identifying, substituting the life of Christ for its own, within and without; by living in him—with him, like him, and through him—so that he may live in that soul and introduce it fully to the reign of the love of the Blessed Trinity in it.

Burning with desire for the kingdom of Christ, which is the kingdom of its Father, the interior soul seeks to remain subject to the action of Christ. It aspires to be as nothing, the nothing of nature, the nothing of itself, so that Christ can take control as its adored Master and Spouse; so that he can reign to the full measure of his overpowering love; so that in him the soul can give itself to the Father, to the fountainhead of Love, of whose reign there shall be no end.

Your kingdom come!

Your Will be Done

VI

YOUR WILL BE DONE on earth as it is in Heaven.

1. It seems strange that the accomplishment of the will of God should depend on our prayer, or has need of our prayer. Can God not do what he pleases?

Of course.

At the same time he has so to say limited his power and will, in creating angels and men. In creating them free, he gave them the ability to resist his will and power. And the wicked angels in their pride revolted against him, while in turn man, in seeking himself rather than God and God's holy will, likewise disobeyed and still disobeys every time his will is not in accord with the will of God.

The will of God is his glory, his reign, and through it our happiness. When therefore we ask that God's will be done on earth as it is in Heaven, we take up again the first petitions of

45

the Our Father and plead for the glory of God and the coming of his kingdom, and by that fact we plead for our own happiness.

We continue too to pray while giving God the first place, seeking God alone and not our own self, even if, in asking that his will be done, it is the grace to do his will for which we are asking him, just as in asking that his kingdom come, it is the realization of our happiness which we implore indirectly.

Thus we preserve the required order, in placing God always in the center and making him the sovereign aim of our prayer and of our own self.

To plead that the will of God be done is to pray that everything on earth as well as in Heaven turn out for his glory. It is to plead that he may reign over every creature and that they all may submit to his dominion.

But it is to plead likewise that this glory be procured by a free act of love, that he may rule over us not by force and tyranny but by the free control of love.

If God has of his own volition put a limit to his power and will, it is because he wished to be adored, loved, and served of our own volition, by free beings, with a will like his, by a free act such as is alone worthy of him.

If therefore we ask that God's will be done,

then what we are asking of him is the grace to submit to his will freely and lovingly, in order thus to procure the more fully his glory and the realization of his reign of love.

Many ask themselves why God, who is almighty, permits war and so many other evils which afflict the earth. Can he not prevent all that, and if he can, why does he not do so?

Ah, that is because, once he created man as the arbiter of his own destiny, he must allow man the freedom and the responsibility of his actions, just as he must let man also bear the consequences of his actions.

It is not God who wishes all the evils which afflict humankind—as little as he wishes Purgatory and Hell. But it is man who wants them. For by the use man makes of his freedom, man at least indirectly wants the evils and sufferings which are the necessary consequence of those voluntary, free actions of his which are not in keeping with the law of what is good.

That is the price we pay for the greatest gift God has made to human nature—for liberty, that attribute of understanding and will which makes up all man's greatness and at the same time provides the greatest possible glory to God in the love and adoration of a free being, of another Himself!

To pray that God's will be done on earth as it is in Heaven, is to plead for his help and light, enabling us to make good use of the great and terrible gift of liberty, making use of it for his greater glory, so that thus the reign of his love may establish itself freely over all men on earth as well as in Heaven.

It is to plead that we may learn humbly to renounce our own will in order to subject it to God's will. For liberty consists in submitting freely to the loving will of the Father, thus freely electing to take our part in the triumph of his glory and the establishment of his reign.

Thus shall we share in his glory and his reign itself, which will constitute our happiness, our eternal bliss.

2. Many think of prayer as a means to bend the will of God to their own will. Filled with desires and aspirations that are often selfish, base and material, they would like by means of their prayer to tie God down to realizing their wishes. Is there any reason, therefore, to be astonished that so many prayers are left unheard? "You ask, and you do not receive, because you ask amiss in the desire to satisfy your passions" (Jas. 4, 3) .

Altogether different is the idea of prayer which Jesus indicates in teaching us to pray,

"Father, your will be done on earth as it is in
Heaven." We do not ask that God do our will,
but that we may have the grace to do his will.
Ah, if all who pray grasped that thought, what
a difference there would be in their disposition!

They would understand that prayer is not a
selfish quest of their personal satisfaction, but an
application of the fundamental principle of perfection, which is renunciation of oneself and
one's own will in order to seek everywhere and
in everything God and his will.

Does this mean to say that it is not at all per-
missible to ask for anything for oneself? By no
means. Jesus himself teaches us in the Our
Father to ask for our daily bread, for the forgiveness of our trespasses, for riddance of our
temptations, and for deliverance from all evil.

But all that is to be in keeping with the
Father's will, and eventually for his love and
glory. It is all asked for with complete resignation to the Father's will, on the condition that
it be conformable to his will and not with our
will if our will be at variance with his will.

Jesus gives us the example of such prayer for
himself with submission to the will of his Father
when in the Garden of Olives, faced with the sufferings which threatened to destroy him, he
prayed humbly: "My Father, if it is possible,

let this chalice pass away from me. But not as I
wish, but as you wish . . . My Father, if this
chalice cannot pass away unless I drink it, may
your will be done" (Mt. 26, 29 and 42).

"May your will be done!" There you have
the last word about every prayer. Not at all in
the spirit of stoical or Moslem fatalism, but as
the act of loving confidence which a child extends to the most loving of fathers, who knows
better than the child what can be truly bene-
ficial to the child, and who always wants what
is best for the child.

Pray, plead with confidence, with persever-
ance, yes—but without ever wishing your own
will to prevail against the will of God, in the
conviction that his will is wiser and better than
yours, that he loves you and that everything
turns out for the good of those who love him!

Once we have grasped that, we are never
disappointed in our prayers. We are always
answered, since after all it is God's will we want;
and if our Father's will is accomplished, so is
our will, being always ready to conform with his.

Just so are our happiness and our desires accomplished thus. For our Father always wishes
our happiness, which is identical with his glory,
while our desires likewise are only for his glory
and our everlasting happiness.

Just in thus giving, as we should, the first place
to God and his will, it is our own good to which
we attain when we pray that the will of our
Father be accomplished. Since God knows better
than we what is good for us, what better can
we ask for ourselves than that his will be accomplished in our behalf, even at the price of a
momentary sacrifice, which at that God will re-
quite a hundredfold.

God is a good father. He desires our welfare,
our sanctity, our eternal bliss, the one thing
after all that matters. "This is the will of God,
your sanctification" (1 Thess. 4, 3).

If God wishes our welfare and our sanctification, is it not clear that to arrive at our happiness and holiness we have only to let God take
over, and to wish whatever he wishes? What
peace, what composure it would provide if we
abandoned ourself thus with confidence into
the arms of our Father, if we saw his holy, ador-
able, loving will in everything befalling us, in
everything that happens!

God wishes it thus, God is permitting it, may
his will be done!

Even if at times nature suffers, deep down in
the soul, supernaturalized by the trial and purified by the suffering, there is the peace and the
perfect joy of St. Francis. Indeed, this is the joy

of all interior souls who are possessed of love
and devotion to the will of God, even then—yes,
above all then—when it crucifies nature.

For it is our welfare, our sanctification which
is at stake—to afford us the chance to give God
greater love, to be the more quickly united with
Christ, transformed into him, made divine in
him, and thus able to make our way back to the
Father through Christ under the loving breath
of the Spirit, there to share in the infinitely
beatifying activity of the Trinity, of the Ocean
of Love Divine.

"Your will be done!" That is not merely a
sigh of resignation.

Oh, no! It is a cry of love and desire; for his
will means himself, and he is Love! To love his
will in all things and wish to realize it in everything, that means to love Love, it means to wish
the total realization of Love, it means to give
oneself over to the action of that Love, which
pacifies, purifies, transforms, makes us divine.

Oh, indeed, dear Lord, not my will but your
will be done. May my will die altogether, so
that I may have no will but yours. In that way
I shall be a solitary spirit with you, transformed
into you, rendered divine in you, in the sole
will of the three Divine Persons, in that Unity
which alone is Love.

Give Us This Day Our Daily Bread

VII

SINCE GOD KNOWS WHATEVER WE have need of even before we ask him for it, why does he wish us to ask him for it? Since he is our father and desires our welfare, is it not enough if we abandon ourselves to his will and wish that it be accomplished?

1. There are people indeed who have acted as if it were useless to pray for what we need, since God knows that without our telling him. And besides, since God has foreseen everything, preordained it and wished it from all eternity, our request cannot in any way change his eternal designs.

So, is it not more simple for us just to submit to the latter without any further desire, and should not our prayer be content to ask for the grace to do his will and submit to his will rather

53

than seek to change it and subject it to our will by means of our prayers?

But ordinary souls have no such misgivings. They are well aware that even if a good father knows what we need, he likes to have us ask for it—it is an act of love and confidence on our part.

What is more, it is an act of humility. Before God we are the last word in indigence. We have nothing but what he gives us. Not to acknowledge that, would be unbearable pride on our part, while to acknowledge it is an act of humility, of self-abasement before God, which both determines him to hear us and leaves us in a condition favorable to receive his gifts, not putting any obstacle in the way of his loving will toward us.

Not to pray, is not to acknowledge our dependence. To pray is to acknowledge our dependence. It is to put us in the only right disposition of the creature toward his Creator.

So, when we say to God, "Give us our daily bread," we recognize our state of need and absolute dependence so far as God is concerned. We exercise ourselves in holy humility. We induce God to give, and dispose ourselves to receive. We practice a child's trust and love.

As for any scruple about predestination and

the eternal, unchangeable will of God, let us leave that to fatalists, to complex souls, and all who would to no purpose work themselves up over a problem that is ill-posed. Plain souls live in the present, in which God himself lives, to whom everything is of the present, and past and future as such do not exist.

But in that present our prayer joined with the will of God can change the course of events, can affect men and things and whatever else is bound up with this earth or the universe or the heavens, without a thought of wishing to change anything in God the unchangeable, and without hindrance from any unchangeable prevision on the part of God. The latter would suppose a past and a future in him to whom everything is present!

Then just let us trustingly ask our Father to give us our daily bread, that is to say, everything we have need of for body and for soul, for ourselves, for our relationship, for all our fellow men.

Always, of course, with full dependence on the will of God and full accord with it. He knows much better than we what would be good bread for us and what rather would be poison.

If we made demands to suit our own will, we

should too often be asking for poison hidden under the deceitful appearances of something good. It would not be for the bread of life, which at times is hidden under the crust of purifying bitter experience and trial.

Let us pray with confidence. Our prayer joined with the will of God can alter the course of events and change the face of the world. It can transform our life. It decides our eternity. "The person who prays, saves his soul; the person who does not pray, is damned."

2. God is well aware of what we need. Nevertheless he wishes us to ask for it in all humility, trust, and love.

But it is unnecessary to specify the object of our prayers. God knows that before we ask for it.

That is why Jesus teaches us to sum up all our needs in a single term, "our daily bread." We thus give expression to our trust in God, as well as to holy simplicity and love of holy poverty. Anyway, why ask for so many things for this life? "Having food and clothing enough, with these let us be content" (1 Tim. 6, 8).

Bread, here, is whatever we need for life, for body and soul. It would be unnecessary and even hazardous to ask for anything else.

And we do well to stress our *daily* bread, to

signify that same trust in God and that same love of holy poverty which are not concerned about tomorrow, according to the words of Jesus, "Do not be anxious about tomorrow, for tomorrow will have its own anxieties. Enough for the day is its own trouble" (Mt. 6, 34) .

What peace, what trust in God is the lot of souls that know how to live and practice the words of Jesus, "Blessed are the poor in spirit, for theirs is the kingdom of Heaven" (Mt. 5, 3) !

On the other hand, how many souls fret and worry and thus forfeit their peace of mind and their life in God, who dwells in peace, because they are disturbed about tomorrow, their future needs, and a thousand imaginary possibilities; because they are preoccupied with the past and the future!

They harry themselves uselessly about a past, which nothing can change anymore, a past which God has forgiven and forgotten, a past which God has wished or at least makes serve the best interests of those who love him: "For those who love God all things work together unto good" (Rom. 8, 28) .

They harry themselves no less uselessly about a future, which likewise is in the hands of God, who will make it serve our welfare. Or it is about imaginary evils which they create for themselves, and which serve no purpose but to increase their worries—things that will never happen at all. "Enough for the day is its own trouble! Give us this day our daily bread!"

If a person has confidence in God and believes in the love God bears toward his children, he has nothing to keep him preoccupied. Anchored in the will of God, who is love, he shares even in this world in God's peace and his changeless eternity. He prays trustingly for his daily bread and abandons himself to God's love as regards past and future.

3. But may we specify our requests in detail as long as they are contained in "our daily bread"?

That is not necessary, since God is well aware of whatever we need before we mention it. Nevertheless that could be useful so far as we are concerned. It can give us the opportunity to correct our natural desires, which incline to take in material goods whereas they should above all extend to supernatural goods. Then too it can impel us to pray with greater fervor and love.

So, we may in all simplicity tell God about our material needs. We can ask him for the bread to maintain the life of the body, for the clothes to protect the body. We can ask for his help in this or that circumstance of our life, for this or that favor, for this particular assistance.

Above all that, however, we will ask for the bread of the soul, of the interior life; for the bread of the Holy Eucharist, which ought to be "daily" with us, like that of the body; for the bread of God's grace, which is the life supplied by the Bread of the Eucharist, the life of Jesus in us, the Divine life, life in God for whom our soul hungers and thirsts.

Imperfect souls find themselves full of a multitude of desires which they bother in vain to satisfy in this world. An interior soul, however, gradually begins to see that at the bottom of all these desires there is one master desire, the mighty desire of the soul which is the love, the possession of God! All the rest is secondary, or it is a fancy of the imagination, "vanity of vanities."

At bottom the soul has only one essential need, a solitary hunger, a solitary thirst, that of God. Our very body, the source of so many desires, when all is said feels (of course in its often deceptive and illusory way) just that voice of man's sole desire: "O God, you are my God, whom I seek from dawn on. My soul thirsts for you, my flesh languishes for you in an arid, parched land without water" (Ps. 62, 2).

The interior soul, which has renounced illusion, finds out that apart from God everything is "arid and parched." It desires but one kind of bread, the bread it will eat all through eternity, the Divine bread, God himself, who is and ever will be the only food of its love and light, he who alone will be able to satisfy its infinite hunger for love and its infinite thirst for light; God who becomes the food and drink of the soul by making the soul share in the eternal generation of the Word and the breath of love of the Holy Spirit in communion with the Word incarnate.

Yes, "man does not live by bread alone but by every word of God" (Lk. 4, 4). "I am the bread of life . . . I am the living bread which has come down from Heaven. If anyone eats of this bread, he shall live forever" (Jn. 6, 35 and 51).

Forgive Us Our Trespasses

VIII

CERTAIN SOULS MAKE all their prayers consist in a continuous plea for forgiveness or a continual examination of concience. They keep recalling sin and the fear of judgment, the fear of Hell or of Purgatory.

1. But our Savior teaches them that the order of our relations with God, including our prayer and the spiritual life, is altogether different.

To think first of all of our sins and keep reflecting on ourself in order to examine our conscience, is quite the contrary of prayer, which consists in forgetting ourself and raising our mind up to Heaven, in getting away from our ego and expanding our soul in God.

Instead of continually reflecting on ourself and thinking of our sins and their punishment, we should give the first place to God, his glory, his kingdom, the triumph of his will, which is the source of love and the bread of the soul.

Only after these considerations should we think of what is opposed to God's glory and reign and love, and beseech God to deliver us from it by cleansing our soul of sin and forgiving us our faults.

To be sure, sin is the one great evil, the only real evil, and remembrance of it ought to be always before our eyes, in order to flee it, to humble ourself for it and repent of it. "My sin is always before me," David says (Ps. 50, 5) in his constant concern for atonement and humiliation.

But we must not let it turn our spirit away from God to concentrate it on ourself, with an egoism and preoccupation with ourself which is the direct opposite of prayer. We must not let it get to the point where it turns our spirit away from God by occupying ourself altogether with ourself and the fear of punishment.

Oh yes, let us fear sin and its consequences, but with filial fear, proceeding from love and confidence in God. Let us fear Purgatory and Hell more out of love of God, and out of displeasure that we cannot give him all our love and glorification, than out of slavish fear of being punished.

The interior soul does not fear the punishment in itself. Conscious of the defilement of sin, the soul rather feels the need of chastisement, and feels impelled to desire the latter in order to be cleansed of its sinfulness and to atone to the Divine justice, so that God's justice may be satisfied.

The only thing it fears is being separated from God, so that it can no longer love him and give him all the glory to which he has a right.

But, suffer so that it can love him all the more, love him with a purer love—oh, indeed!

Rather than for fear of Hell or Purgatory, it is for love of the glory and love of God and for the sake of atoning purification that the interior soul prays with all its heart, "Forgive us our debts."

And if it often repeats that cry of remorse, that cry for deliverance, it is because that cry is at the same time a cry of confidence, love, and desire, which turns the soul back on itself, on examination of conscience and on contrition and abasement only to take occasion once again of giving itself so much the more to God and expanding its life in God in the desire for purification—a purification brought about far sooner by communion with God than by fear and gloomy reflection.

It is of a kind father that the interior soul seeks forgiveness, and that thought opens its heart for a cry of confidence and love that is stronger than its fear of the Judge. Recalling the Prodigal Son, it proceeds to cast itself into the arms of its Father. There it finds its purification in giving him greater joy than can be given him by the ninety-nine who have no need of repentance (Lk. 15, 7).

2. The great commandment of Jesus, "the new commandment," is love. And if love must accompany all the life of a Christian, it certainly must characterize prayer as taught by Christ, prayer, which constitutes the chief activity of love.

As a matter of fact, the entire Our Father is a reaction against that egoism of man which causes a person to concentrate on himself and think of his own interests in preference to everything else.

Jesus, on the other hand, teaches us to get out of ourself and expand in God. The entire first part of the Our Father manifests that enlargement in God, that giving of the foremost place to God and his glory, which is the proper order of charity as contained in the chief commandment of love: "Love the Lord your God with all your heart, with all your soul, and with all your mind. That is the greatest and the foremost commandment" (Mt. 22, 37).

But the second is similar to it: "Love your neighbor as yourself" (ib. 39).

The love of God cannot be separated from the love of our neighbor. Not to love our neighbor is not to love God, for in a sense our neighbor is part of God, since he is a member of Christ and through him and in him of God himself; and to separate oneself from a member of Christ is to separate oneself from Christ himself, and so to separate oneself from God.

We cannot love God except in Christ, in unison with Christ. That is why our Savior wishes that our prayer, which is an act of the love of God in Christ, be performed in Christ's name and in the name of all his members, in the name of the entire Christ.

In his name therefore we say: *"Our* Father, give *us* this day *our* daily bread, forgive *us our* trespasses."

Yes, selfishness, the enemy of charity and unity, must be excluded from our prayer, and charity must be joined with it, to that extent that God makes the forgiveness of our sins depend on the forgiveness we accord to our brothers.

"Forgive us our trespasses as we forgive those

who trespass against us." "For if you forgive men their offenses, your heavenly Father will also forgive your offenses. But if you do not forgive men, neither will your Father forgive you your offenses" (Mt. 6, 14-15).

So great, so important is the second commandment, of pardon and love of neighbor, that without that love there can be no love of God and no pardon at the hands of God! Pardoning is one of the acts of love. No pardon, no love. And there is only one love: it is the love of God, and of everything and everybody in God.

How badly therefore those people deceive themselves who think they are approaching God in their prayer and believe they love him and are enjoying his forgiveness, while they are retaining hatred and rancor in their heart against their neighbor!

Give pardon and you will be pardoned, love your neighbor and you will be loved by God, for he will pardon you only if you pardon, and will love you only if you love him by loving your neighbor, who is a member of Christ, a member of God.

Why is it that so many devout souls make no progress at all in holiness and union with God? Ah, that is because they think they can love God

without loving their neighbor; without giving
up their criticisms, their rash judgments, their
back-biting, their slanderous talk; without prac-
ticing forbearance and forgiveness toward their
neighbor. "Judge not, that you may not be
judged" (Mt. 7, 2).

A soul that is truly interior, feels within itself
treasures of forbearance and forgiveness, taken
up from the Heart of Jesus, who lives in such a
soul. In that Heart and from it the soul lives,
in the only love which avails to weld the two
commandments so similar to each other.

Such a soul always enjoys pardon, purification, and life in the love of God, because it does
not judge, but always pardons others, in keeping
with what Jesus commanded.

For when Peter came up to our Lord and said:
"Lord, how often shall my brother sin against
me and I forgive him? Maybe seven times?"
Jesus said to him: "I do not say to you seven
times, but seventy times seven" (Mt. 18, 21-22).
That means, all the time.

That, therefore, is how far charity extends.
That is the condition on which we must obtain
pardon, inasmuch as anybody who cannot find
it in himself to give pardon, cannot say the Our
Father without asking judgment on himself.

Dreadful demand of love! But at the same time, what an easy well-spring of pardon, what a fountainhead of charity, peace, and harmony for all the world, if everybody understood the law of forgiveness, if everybody undertsood how to translate the Our Father into practice!

Lead Us Not into Temptation

IX

THE WORDS "Lead us not into temptation," have often been used as a point of departure for their heresy by persons who saw in them a proof that certain people are predestined to evil and to Hell regardless of their will in the matter. As if God led them into temptation to have them succumb to it so that he could damn them!

1. St. James (1, 13-15) had given the answer to such persons in advance:

"Let no man say, when he is tempted, that he is tempted by God. For God is no way tempted to evil and he himself tempts no one. But everyone is tempted by being drawn away and enticed by his own passion. Then when passion has conceived, it brings forth sin, but when sin has matured, it begets death."

Then why should we beseech God not to lead

69

us into temptation, if he does not tempt any-body?

The Fathers have sought to make the difficulty clear by giving the words a different turn, a para-phrase. Thus Tertullian puts it: "Do not permit us to be led into temptation." St. Cyprian and St. Augustine give the same explanation, while St. Jerome translates the words: "Lead us not into a temptation beyond our strength."

A current translation of the words in other languages, as in French, is, "Do not let us suc-cumb to temptation," and that is the most natural meaning of the words, in any case the meaning true to fact.

Temptation itself is not sin, and God can permit it for our good. So all we do is ask him not to let us succumb to it, but give us the grace to overcome it, so that we do not offend him but rather merit Heaven by our victory in the test.

It is a fact that the life of man is a "tempta-tion" in the sense of a trial or test (at bottom, that is what the term means), to which man must be subjected in order to determine whether he shall be worthy of Heaven or of Hell. Inordi-nate concupiscence is a consequence of sin, but the test or "temptation," is there independently of any fall, had to be there before any fall.

Was it not as a result of such a test by the demon of curiosity, desire and pride that Eve looked at the fruit, craved it, ate it, and gave it to Adam to eat? Were not the angels themselves thus tested before their fall into Hell or their ascent into Heaven?

Whoever is not thus tested, has no chance to earn merits and to conquer, no chance to acquire virtues, which are a habit, that is, a facile accomplishment of the soul won by repeated victory over temptation.

Does that, however, mean that we must hunt up temptation in order to have the chance to conquer, to earn merits, to acquire virtue?

No indeed. That would be presumption and pride. That would be tempting God and presuming on our strength, and in such case, to punish and humble us, God could let us succumb to temptation. He that loves danger, shall perish in it.

It is in that sense that we can beseech God not "to lead us into temptation," that is, not to permit that we ever be tempted beyond our feeble powers.

God therefore permits temptation in order to exercise our strength, to have us grow in virtue, and to acquire merits for Heaven.

We, however, need not be afraid of it as long

as we remain humbly aware of our weakness
while relying on the grace which God will give
us in proportion to the temptation. "God is
faithful, and will not permit you to be tempted
beyond your strength, but with the temptation
will also give you a way out, that you may be
able to bear it" (1 Cor. 10, 13).

2. Only, we must be humble enough to recognize that without God we can do nothing.
"God resists the proud, but gives his grace to the
humble" (Jas. 4, 6).

To St. Paul, who begged the Lord insistently
to be delivered from his temptation, God prom-
ised the grace of surmounting the temptation
instead of taking it from him. "Concerning it
I thrice besought the Lord that it might leave
me, and he said to me, My grace is sufficient for
you, for strength is made perfect in weakness"
(2 Cor. 12, 8-9).

The great benefit of temptation is just this
that it keeps us humble, giving God all the glory
and merit of our actions. In it God teaches us
to realize all our misery, weakness, and corrup-
tion, so that we learn not to count on ourselves
and our strength, but on him alone.

Once we are thus fully aware of our nothingness and weakness, God can proceed to deal with
us without having our ego interfere with any

pretensions of merit of its own. He will be able to achieve in us the work of purifying and transforming our soul and making it divine, so that in it all his glory will shine forth, without having us attribute anything to ourself. Trial will have demonstrated our nothingness and our impotence to do anything good of ourself.

Thus, though we must not look for temptation, though we must rather avoid it in the spirit of holy fear and humility, we must not on the other hand worry if God sends it to us, nor look upon it as a punishment, or as a sign of spiritual failure, or of abandonment on the part of God.

Of course, if any souls through their own fault expose themselves to temptation, the worry this causes them later on may be a punishment for their lack of prudence, their inquisitiveness, or their presumption.

As for others, however—those who flee from temptation and are nevertheless beset by it— let them have no fear: the temptation will serve for their perfection. It can prove a grace of God and a source of spiritual progress.

There are middling souls which are never or only rarely tempted. On the other hand, there are souls far advanced in the interior life which are so to say crushed under the weight of their

temptations—temptations against faith, hope,
charity; temptations to hatred, blasphemy, glut-
tony, impurity.

Such temptations serve to deepen their humility; to purify them of every trace of pride,
attachment to creatures and quest of personal
gratification; to despoil them of all human support in order to precipitate them into the arms
of God in pure supernatural faith; to reduce
them to nothing in their awareness of their
nothingness, so that God alone can be all in
all to them.

In praying, "Lead us not into temptation,"
the soul may indeed in all humility ask God
to be delivered from the temptation, provided
it remains disposed to bear the temptation as
long as God pleases. In this regard, as with any
other cross, the soul says to God what Jesus
said: If it is possible, remove it from me, yet
not as I wish, but as you wish.

What the soul asks foremost, is the grace not
to succumb under the pressure of temptation,
not to fail in the trial, but to make it serve the
designs of almighty God, that is, his greater
honor and glory, the soul's own welfare and
that of so many other souls who are in need of
help to survive temptation.

In this way too the Communion of the Saints

and the Mystical Body are manifested: God has strong souls undergo trials that weaker souls could not endure. Are we not told that the Curé of Ars took upon himself the temptations and trials of penitents who had previously always given way under them and who thereafter were completely free of them?

"Lead *us* not into temptation!" As with the other petitions, it is not for himself alone that the petitioner formulates his plea, but it is in the name of everybody, the stronger among them being ready to help bear the burdens of the weaker, while the weaker ask God to let them find support in the stronger. That too is characteristic of the charity governing the worldwide expanse of the kingdom of Divine love.

Deliver Us from Evil

X

EVIL IS WHATEVER is opposed to the kingdom of God, to our welfare, happiness, and eternal bliss.

This last petition of the Our Father is therefore a cry for deliverance, a forceful aspiration toward freedom, from whatever oppresses us and causes us suffering, an impulse toward Heaven and toward eternity, which alone will prove genuine deliverance from evil.

1. Evil is suffering, whether moral or physical, both personal suffering and the suffering we share intimately with others.

It includes everything that causes us to suffer —sickness and death, cold and heat, hunger and thirst; cravings unsatisfied and the boredom of oversatisfaction; hatred which upsets the soul and love which finds no response; war and all the upheavals of the physical and moral order in the world, and so forth.

Of all that we ask God to be delivered, while we yearn for Paradise, for well established order, for peace, for mutual charity; with our desires ever satisfied yet without being glutted; with the master desire for the eternal welfare of our body and soul.

But just as there is only one genuine happiness, that of Heaven, so there is only one true evil. That evil consists in whatever is opposed to Heaven and union with God, in sin.

So, when we implore God to deliver us from evil, it is above all from sin that we beg to be delivered. Sin is the source of all evils. It is the one thing that is evil in itself, because it is the one thing that deprives us of our true good, of God.

God had created man to live in a paradise on earth. All our evils came as a consequence of sin. But apart from sin, which is disobedience toward God, partial or total separation from God, and comparative or unconditional rebellion against God, all other evils amount to nothing except that in the intentions of God they are meant to serve for man's welfare.

God permits evil only with a view to what is good. He permits sin itself only with a view to the infinite recompense of those who will stand the test of life and will thus deserve Heaven. He permits all other evils only to restore the balance of his justice, which is outraged by sin, and in order to rescue man from sin.

The very thought of Hell itself is meant to waken in man a wholesome fear regarding sin. Purgatory is there to cleanse man from sin in order to fit him for the presence of God, the infinitely Pure.

Suffering, together with all the evils which afflict man, serves to atone for his faults, to purify his soul, to realize in the latter the kingdom of God and help it measure up to God's purity with the abundance of his grace.

When therefore we beseech God to deliver us from evil, it is above all from sin and Hell that we should think of being preserved.

As for other evils, evils of this world, we may likewise humbly ask to be delivered from them, but always in full accord with the will of God. That means, if they are to serve for our welfare and purification, we will accept them cheerfully, only asking God that they do not exceed our strength and that God may give us the grace to make good use of them, for his glory, and for the welfare of our soul and that of our fellow men, as members of the Mystical Body and the Communion of the Saints.

2. In their ardent thirst for purification, and

also by reason of their loving desire to share in
the sufferings of Christ for the redemption of
souls, the saints often reach the point where
they no longer ask for deliverance from physical
evil but actually desire it, yes they pray for suffering as the most desirable of blessings!

When St. Teresa prayed, "Lord, let me suffer,
or die!" or St. Mary Magdalene de' Pazzi prayed,
"Lord, let me not die but suffer!" they went
through an experience common to interior souls
at a certain stage of the spiritual life.

There are souls that enter so deeply into the
value of love for suffering, that their eagerness
to possess God in the full light of Heaven is tem-
pered by the thought that in Heaven they will
have no opportunity to possess the great blessing
of suffering!

The world has no understanding for that great
love of suffering. To the world that is the only
evil, and all the world's preferences go out to
sin, although after all it is the latter which is
unadulterated evil. That is how blind nature
can be when it lacks the enlightenment of grace
by means of supernatural charity.

On the other hand, under the light and attrac-
tion of grace the soul is at times so thoroughly
penetrated with the need of purifying itself of
sin by means of suffering, in order to draw nearer

to God, that suffering appears to it to be the
one true blessing, the most desirable of blessings.

As said, under inspiration from above, in full
accord with obedience and the will of God, and
at the same time in all humility and conscious
of their weakness, certain souls reach the point
where they pray, not for deliverance from suffering, but for the grace of suffering.

They appreciate so fully that the love, the joy,
the bliss of eternity are the fruits of suffering
here below, that they regret the end of it in
Heaven, since it will mean too the end of their
advancement in love.

Of course, that regret will not continue in
Heaven, because there, completely satisfied according to its particular capacity, every soul will
enjoy the fulness of bliss amid freedom from
all evils.

That is why the interior soul, filled as it is
with love of the cross as the means of its purification and redemption, in its desire for fulness
of the love of God cries out with St. Paul: "I
am hard pressed on both sides—I desire to depart
and to be with Christ, a lot by far the better; at
the same time to stay on in the flesh, as being
more necessary for your sake" (Phil. 1, 23-24).

When the soul prays, "Deliver us from evil,"
it voices its desire to go to Heaven with Christ

and its desire to be thus delivered from all evil amid the infinite joy of eternity. But first it voices its desire to be delivered from the only evil that counts, from sin and its damaging effects.

As for the rest, it abandons itself to the will of God. For his will is a will full of love for us. His will is our greatest blessing. In his will we shall have deliverance from genuine evil. His will is our joy everlasting, unto his honor and his love.

Amen

XI

A S A RULE THE CHURCH reserves her prayers for the celebrating or officiating priest to say. The rest, the faithful, content themselves with saying "Amen, so be it."

That Amen sums up the whole prayer. It signifies the full accord of all with the prayer of the Church, the prayer of Christ. The Amen of the Our Father carries the soul up again to our Father, who is in the Heavens. It wishes to chant his glory, to call for the coming of his kingdom. It signifies giving full assent to his will in our craving for our daily bread, for pardon, for deliverance from temptation, and from all evil.

Just as the word "Father," which begins the prayer, so the closing "Amen" comprises our entire prayer. It does not need a lot of words. A single word, a glance, a sigh is enough to accomplish our elevation to God, to give expression to our desire and our accord with his will.

Non-Catholics have been known to cast asper-
sions on Catholic prayer as being unintelligible,
or made in a foreign language. They have sought
to replace it with improvised prayer of their
own, presumably more in keeping with good
sense, more understandable, and more completely human.

In doing so, they have only fallen into a form
of rationalism and naturalism which are indeed
more human but also void of the Divine and of
everything supernatural, which should be the
life of our prayer and of all our interior life.

When we pray supernaturally, it is not we
who are saying the prayer, but Jesus in us, and
we only insofar as we are in him. Our prayer is
essentially elevation of ourselves in him toward
the Father in the Holy Ghost. It is accord
with him, with his prayer, with his adoration,
with his petition.

For that reason it is not necessary that we com-
prehend, be conscious of, or detail our needs.
God knows them well enough and Jesus in his
Spirit knows better than we do what we should
ask for.

For that reason, furthermore, our prayer is
much rather an assent to Christ's prayer than
a plea in our name, and it is a frame of mind

rather than a fine combination of phrases. It is union with God in Christ, with our mind rising up to him, a matter of loving activity.

But for the latter, in order to love, words are not necessary. Just a single word is enough, such as saying "Father," or "Amen."

Making our life a continuous amen to the will of God—that is to keep praying always. It is to be perfect. It is to attain to sanctity, for our sanctification is the will of God.

To the extent that words are necessary or rather useful to produce and maintain that state of soul in us—and for most of us words serve that purpose—let us make use of the beautiful formula of the Our Father, or of the Psalms, or of liturgical prayers. Let us say them in union with Christ, and the Holy Spirit who has inspired them, without being troubled about our dryness or any involuntary distractions.

What consolation there is in this rule for such people as have to fight against distractions continually! What consolation for those who suffer from dryness and find no relish in any kind of prayer! What consolation for those who, though not afflicted with dryness, find no nourishment in any words and long for a God-pleasing way to pray without human words!

What consolation for anybody, to be aware

that beyond their distractions, their dryness, the words they might use, Jesus is there with his Spirit to pray in them, in the depths of their soul, with a Divine prayer that is wordless, prayer that is the very essence of prayer, since it is the Son giving himself to the Father for them in the loving breath of the Holy Spirit!

Therefore, to pray well it suffices for us to unite ourselves — notwithstanding distractions and in spite of dryness—with Jesus in the depth of our soul; to permit him to be all our prayer, he in us and we in him; to unite ourselves in thought and sentiment, or simply in will and intention, with Jesus' way of praying, which is that of the Our Father, with its prayer of adoration and praise, of desire for God's kingdom, of union of our will with that of the Father; its prayer of petition for our daily bread, for pardon of our offenses, and for deliverance from evil.

Let us unite ourselves with Jesus and his intentions, be it with or without words, in that essential word addressed by the Son to the Father, which is "Abba—Father"; the word in which the Son says everything there is to be said, and gives himself, and us in him, to the Father, with the sentiments expressed in the Our Father.

Thus our prayer will always be a good and perfect prayer. It will constitute a perfect, continuous gift of our love and adoration, of continuous prayer. It will be turning our life into a living Our Father made up of all we do day by day.

Such prayer in Jesus comprises all the prayers that can be said; for it expresses all the proper sentiments in perfect order. And since, in praying in Jesus and with Jesus, we pray with all the Mystical Body, we pray as the entire Mystical Body in its graded ascent to the Father himself in Jesus.

We pray with all the holy souls of the Church Militant, Suffering, and Triumphant; with the angels, who are its first members; and with the glorious Virgin Mary, who is its blessed Mother; and with Christ, who is its Head and Mediator.

Thus we unite all the Mystical Body with the Father in that eternal gift of Love which is the Holy Ghost returning to establish the ultimate of Unity.

The Our Father of St. Francis

APPENDIX

THERE HAS BEEN some discussion, notably in these latter years, as to whether the spirit of St. Francis was Christocentric, that is, directed toward Christ as its particular center, and not rather directed toward the Father. There are advocates of both positions.

As for ourself, either position is correct provided they are not understood as excluding each other but duly subordinated to each other. It is certain that St. Francis made Christ, and union and identification with Christ, the center and foundation of all his life. But it is no less certain that he did not halt at Christ, but went with him and in him to the Father.

From the outset of his religious life, when he first gave himself up altogether to Christ, he clearly manifested his impulse toward the Father. For when his earthly father demanded the restitution of what goods of his Francis had distrib-

uted to the poor, Francis, impelled by an excess
of love for holy poverty, stripped himself of his
very clothes to return them to his father, saying:

"Listen, all, and note it well. Up till now I
have called Peter Bernardone my father. But
as I have now determined to serve God, I herewith give back to him the money which has given
me so much trouble and likewise the clothes I
have received from him, so that hereafter I can
say with fuller truth, 'Our Father, who are in
Heaven,' and no longer, 'My father, Peter Bernardone.' Till now I have appealed to my
father here on earth; from now on I shall be able
to say with full confidence: 'Our Father, who
are in Heaven, with whom I have laid by all my
treasure'" (St. Bonaventure, Leg. Maj. 2).

Have we not right here all that impulse of love
for the Father, from whom comes every perfect
gift, and to whom everything must be lovingly
returned? That is what is expressed in St. Francis' Paraphrase of the Our Father, which follows
herewith*:

"Our Father most holy: our Creator, our Re-
deemer and Savior, our Comforter.

---

*A note in the Assisi MS. of the saint's writings tells that
St. Francis said the Our Father together with other praises of
God before each Hour of the Breviary as well as before saying
the Little Office of the Blessed Virgin. The Paraphrase and the
Praises are No. 36 in Meyer, *The Words of St. Francis*, Fran-
ciscan Herald Press.—The Translator.

"Who are in Heaven: in the angels and the saints, giving them light to know you, since you, O Lord, are Light; setting them afire to love you, since you, O Lord, are Love; abiding in them and filling them for their bliss, since you, O Lord, are the sovereign good, the eternal good, from which everything good has its being and without which there is nothing good.

"Hallowed be your name: may we grow in our knowledge of you, that we may appreciate the width of your favors and the length of your promises to us, as well as the utter height of your majesty and the depth of your judgments (cf. Eph. 3, 18).

"Your kingdom come: so that you may rule in us through grace and have us get to your kingdom, where the sight of you is clear, love of you is perfect, association with you is full of bliss, and enjoyment of you is eternal.

"Your will be done on earth as it is in Heaven: so that we may love you with all our heart by always keeping you in mind; with all our soul by always longing for you; with all our mind by directing all our intentions to you and seeking your glory in everything; and with all our strength by exerting all the forces and faculties of soul and body in your loving service and in nothing else. So may we love our neighbors

as ourselves, by getting them all so far as we can to love you, by being as glad at the good fortune of others as at our own, while feeling for their misfortune, and giving no offense to anybody (cf. 2 Cor. 6, 3) .

*"Give us this day—*so that we will remember, understand and respect the love he bore for us and all he said and did and endured for us— *our daily bread—*your beloved Son, our Lord Jesus Christ.

"And forgive us our debts: in your unutterable mercy, in virtue of the suffering of your beloved Son, our Lord Jesus Christ, and at the merits and intercession of the blessed Virgin Mary, and all your elect.

"As we forgive our debtors: and what we do not fully forgive, do you, O Lord, make us forgive fully, so that for your sake we may truly love our enemies and devotedly intercede with you for them, giving nobody evil in return for evil and trying to be helpful toward everybody in your name.

"And lead us not into temptation: neither hidden nor apparent, neither sudden nor persistent.

"But deliver us from evil: past, present, and future. Amen.

"Glory be to the Father," etc.

THE END.